# Gardens of the Heart

◇

*A Special Gift for*

*From*

# GARDENS OF THE HEART

Formerly published under the title,
*The Fruit of the Spirit*

Printed in Hong Kong

ISBN 0-915720-59-0

# Gardens
## of the
# Heart

◆

*Leroy Brownlow*

*Brownlow*

Brownlow Publishing Company, Inc,

## OTHER BROWNLOW GIFT BOOKS

*A Few Hallelujahs for Your Ho-Hums*
*A Psalm in My Heart*
*As a Man Thinketh*
*Better Than Medicine—A Merry Heart*
*Children Won't Wait*
*Flowers for Mother*
*Flowers for You*
*Flowers of Friendship*
*Flowers That Never Fade*
*For Mom With Love*
*Give Us This Day*
*Grandpa Was a Preacher*
*It's a One-derful Life*
*Jesus Wept*
*Just Between Friends*
*Leaves of Gold*
*Love Is Forever*
*Making the Most of Life*
*The Greatest Thing in the World*
*The Other Wise Man*
*Thoughts of Gold—Wisdom for Living*
*Today and Forever*
*Today Is Mine*
*University of Hard Knocks*
*Your Special Day*

# CONTENTS

# FOREWORD

> But the fruit of the Spirit is love, joy, peace, longsuffering, kindness, goodness, faithfulness, meekness, self-control...
> —Galatians 5:22,23

*W*ithin each of us lies a garden of the heart — a place where God can plant, water, cultivate and gently nurture a beautiful harvest of character. But it is not just any harvest, it is a harvest of love, joy, peace, longsuffering, kindness, goodness, faithfulness, meekness and self-control. Yes, He plants and waters the fruit of the Spirit.

As we allow our hearts and minds to become God's garden, we shall find that we will be blessed beyond all expectation. Our lives will become filled with His qualities, His attributes. The garden will become like the Gardener. And that is God's greatest desire — for us to become like Him.

GARDENS OF THE HEART

LOVE & LOVE & LOVE & LOVE & LOVE & LOVE & LOVE & LOVE

GARDENS OF THE HEART

Ah, what is life? 'Tis more than
breathing and counting birthdays.
More than footprints on the sands
of time. More than a pilgrimage
through this mortal world.

#  LOVE

It is an experience marked by deeds, not days; by thoughts, not time; by feelings, not numbers on a calendar. And the one feeling that does more to add meaning, fulness, stature, zest and satisfaction, to our days is love. So he who loves most lives most. Without it, the human heart becomes an aching void, ever enlarging by the multiplying misdirections and disappointments that are so visible in our restless society.

Dear reader, if you have failed to kindle and keep burning the radiance of love in your heart, you have sentenced yourself to a cold and heartless existence. Yes, you have missed out on the most satisfying and rewarding quality in all the world. Undoubtedly, you have fallen short of an indescribable joy that is impossible to have apart from love. Also, you have come up lacking a lovely magnetism that would draw the world to your presence, for human beings naturally gravitate toward those with loving hearts. You are the loser, but so is the world; for the whole wide world needs love. For love is the director that brings together and reconciles the discordant notes in our jangling society and converts them into a beautiful harmony.

Truly, love is the sweetest thing that ever grew in a human heart.

Attesting to its breadth and length, depth and height, beauty and goodness, helpfulness and holiness, the very word picked by the Holy Spirit to describe God is love. John, inspired by the Holy Spirit, simply and briefly put it this way:

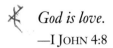 *God is love.*
—I JOHN 4:8

In those three words we have a whole book. Yea, more than a book. A whole library!

Now, we do not wonder why love heads the list of the fruits of the Spirit (Galatians 5:22,23). It is so inclusive that all of the other praiseworthy fruits mentioned in the passage can be considered as distinct components of love. It is easy to view it as such a broad embodiment when we read I Corinthians 13 and consider all the things that Paul says love is.

◆ *So much is included in this word—love.* Everything that is good and beneficial. It is the highest and worthiest virtue. There is nothing low or cheap about love. This is why God is called *love.* Thus the inference is clear—the more love you have, the more godly you are.

Love's superiority is further seen in that the Two Great Commandments are based on love:

> *Thou shalt love the Lord thy God*
> *With all thy heart,*
> *And with all thy soul,*
> *And with all thy mind.*
> *This is the first and great commandment.*
> *And the second is like unto it,*
> *Thou shalt love thy neighbor as thyself.*
> —MATTHEW 22:37-39

Since the greatest commandments are founded on love, then it follows that love must be the greatest of all attributes.

Love is so all-inclusive and all-embracing of compounded goodness that the Apostle Paul put it ahead of even faith and hope. He declared:

*But now abideth faith, hope, love, these three;*
*and the greatest of these is love.*
—I CORINTHIANS 13:13

Why? Because where there is love, there is faith and there is hope. So love is greater than either, for the whole is always greater than its parts. Just like the foot is greater than its toes, and the hand is greater than its fingers.

So studying the exalted topic of love takes us to the top of the world where everything is well-behaved, par excellent and exceptionally beneficent.

◆ *From the immortal Thirteenth Chapter of I Corinthians we learn that:* "Love suffereth long"—patient; "and is kind"—kind behavior; "love envieth not"—generous; "love vaunteth not itself, is not puffed up"—humble; "doth not behave itself unseemly"—courteous; "seeketh not her own"—unselfish; "is not easily provoked"—mild tempered; "thinketh no evil"—guileless; "rejoiceth not in iniquity, but rejoiceth in the truth"—sincere; "beareth all things"—tolerant; "believeth all things"—believing; "hopeth all things"—hopeful; "endureth all things"—enduring; "love never faileth"—unfailing. What a blessed list of characteristics for which to strive. And the remarkable thing is, they are all found in one word—*love*. Just fill your heart with love and all these traits that make the most attractive and laudable personality will automatically develop. Love does it.

This is why the person with a loving heart—no hate, no bitterness, no resentment—excels all the rest and attains the highest peak of living.

> *Ah, how skillful grows the hand*
> *That obeyed Love's command!*
> *And he who followeth Love's behest*
> *Far excelleth all the rest.*

—HENRY WADSWORTH LONGFELLOW

◆ *The world's most effective transforming power is love.* It is the lofty force that could cure the many ills in our society: Ills in religion because love has taken a back pew or moved out entirely. Ills in business because love has been replaced by greed. Ills in society because of misplaced love—love of self rather than the other fellow. Ills in family life because love has lost its dominance and selfishness has lifted its head. Indeed, the unfailing cure for self-interest is love. For love "seeketh not her own."

In a farm family in which death took both parents in a short time, five children were left to make their own way. The eldest was a girl eighteen years of age who was determined to keep the orphan family together. On her rested the responsibility of being both mother and father to the young ones. Work!

Work! Work! She had to work from early morning until late at night: plowing, planting, harvesting, gardening, milking, canning, cooking, sewing, laundering and the doing of a hundred other things. In time, it broke her health; she developed tuberculosis where it finally reached its last stages. Realizing that life was gradually ebbing away, she said to the minister who often visited her, "I know it won't be long until I reach the end and it seems I've done so little in life. I don't know what I'm going to tell the Lord for not doing more." The preacher said, "Don't tell Him anything. Just show Him your hands."

Those were unselfish hands. The hands of love. A love so great that it had completely forgotten self.

Instead of self-centeredly seeking to get, to exploit and to take advantage of others, love—unselfish love—gives and gives and gives. For this is love's way.

> *Love ever gives—*
> *Forgives—outlives—*
> *And ever stands*
> *With open hands.*
> *And while it lives—*
> *It gives*
> *For this is love's prerogative—*

*To give—and give—and give.*
—JOHN OXENHAM

Yes, definitely, one of love's most appreciated attributes is its unselfish, sacrificial nature. It will live and die for its love. And in the latter instance, it is love at its fullest. For there is no more selfless gift than one's own life. The Bible holds this maxim before us: "Greater love hath no man than this, that a man lay down his life for his friends" (John 15:13).

Since love is an emotion regulated by the lover, not the one being loved, then it is possible for one to love everybody, even enemies. Actually, it is more than a possibility; it is a definite command given by Jesus:

> *But I say unto you,*
> *Love your enemies,*
> *Bless them that curse you,*
> *Do good to them that hate you,*
> *And pray for them which despitefully*
>   *use you and persecute you.*
> —MATTHEW 5:44

Obedience to this command is within the reach of all, because love is a feeling that manifests itself in keeping with who we are, not what the other person is. This is why God loves everybody—not that everybody is lovable. Hence, we see that it is not unreasonable to love an enemy. And the more we do it, the more we are changed into the likeness of God.

From both the Biblical and philosophical viewpoints we see the wisdom of loving our enemies. Meeting enmity with enmity aggravates and multiplies the problem. Hating them back brings only more hate and strife and heartbreak. Since like begets like and reaping depends on sowing, then there is a chance that loving an enemy may break through that hard, calloused crust of ill will and convert it into love and thereby change the order of events. Maybe not. But can. For the principle of reciprocal love is an accepted fact and is stated in the Bible:

*We love him, because he first loved us.*
—I JOHN 4:19

But if you should not be able to love the animosity out of an enemy, you still have triumphed; you have won over a lower inclination and have become better for having tried. And happier. Because there is a greater blessing in loving than in being loved. This being true, remember—there is no wasted love.

*Talk not of wasted affection, affection*
*never was wasted;*
*If it enrich not the heart of another,*
*its waters, returning*

*Back to their springs, like the rain,*
*Shall fill them full of refreshment.*
—HENRY WADSWORTH LONGFELLOW

◆ *As we evaluate love's might let us keep in mind that love has a warmth* that exerts more power than hate's cold force. In keeping with this thought, there is a fable concerning an argument between the Wind and the Sun as to which could compel a man the quickest to remove his coat. The Wind got busy and blew its strong blast. But the man only drew his cloak all the tighter around him. Then the Sun with a different approach shone bright and warm upon the man, and he voluntarily removed his coat. The moral is: the best way to get people to do what you wish is to love them into it. Scolding and scoffing, tantalizing and threatening may cause them to only cloak themselves against you. A better way is to love them—speak considerately and act kindly. Honey catches more flies than vinegar.

◆ *Another sweet virtue of love is its inclination to be blind to faults.* Hence, love brings new sight to old eyes. It lets you see the best in a person. Unless we are careful, what we see may be more in the eye of the beholder than in the object. Then how important it is that the viewer look through the heart lenses of love.

*Love to faults is always blind,*
*Always is to joy inclin'd,*
*Lawless, wing'd, and unconfin'd,*
*And breaks all chains from every mind.*
—WILLIAM BLAKE

And when it does recognize imperfection, *it does not vary* for it is blind to indicting causes.

*Love is not love*
*Which alters when it alteration finds,*
*Or bends with the remover to remove:*
*O, no! is an ever-fixed mark*
*That looks on tempests and is never shaken.*
—WILLIAM SHAKESPEARE

Instead of altering, love mercifully curtains the weakness.

*For love covereth a multitude of sins.*
—I PETER 4:8

◆ *It is not trite, therefore, to say that love will solve our problems,* no more stereotyped than to say that food sustains life. Without food man dies; and without love man dies a death worse than physical. The reason—man is a creature in need of love. His heart cries out for affection, affection to give and affection to receive. He needs to love and he needs to be loved. Nothing will adequately take its place.

*Better is a dinner of herbs where love is,*
*than a stalled ox and hatred within.*
—PROVERBS 15:17

Let us, therefore never doubt the efficacy and utility of love.

*Doubt, if you will, the being who loves you,*
*Woman or dog, but never doubt love itself.*
—ALFRED DE MUSSET

◆ *Now let us bear in mind that love—this beautiful quality—is available to all* if all will open their hearts to God and allow it to grow. It is not the exclusive property of the educated nor the wealthy nor the prestigious. It does not have to come in a luxury package. Neither does it have to be wrapped in a college diploma. It is something each, regardless of station in life, can speak and demonstrate in his or her own way; and, after all, that simple heart language is the most beautiful poetry and the grandest eloquence. Furthermore, there has never been a stronger statement on love than the simple expression, "I love you." Love is simple. And its power and joy are the same in all.

*Seas have their source, and so have shallow springs;*
*And love is love, in beggars as in kings.*
—SIR EDWARD DYER

GARDENS OF THE HEART

JOY · JOY · JOY · JOY · JOY · JOY

JOY · JOY · JOY · JOY · JOY · JOY

GARDENS OF THE HEART

*Melancholy, sadness and despair should have no home in religion. They are not the fruits of the Spirit; to the contrary, joy is.*

# 2  JOY

Sow to the Spirit and you shall reap (Galatians 6:8), and one of the reapings is happiness. So the most basic reason for joy is the Spirit, His directions, His blessings and His promises.

◆ *It is unfortunate that some have thought that religion comes with a sad face wrapped with a frown.* And this perversion of religion and miscarriage of life has twisted the thinking of many people and robbed them of the joy the Spirit intended for them to have.

A sad face, therefore, is not a very good recommendation of Christianity. A world of sinners, frustrated with troubles, has enough sadness without having more poured on it by the misguided children of God.

◆ *Joy is positive and comes from optimism.* Sadness is negative, emanates from pessimism. And speaking of joy, the pessi*mist* it.

Now from the multitudinous ranks of the unhappy we hear the anxious question: "How can you be optimistic and cheerful in view of the ever-changing fortunes of life? Broken health, loss of job, betrayal by a friend, exploitation by others, failure to meet goals, etc."

◆ *Troubles! troubles! and the handling of them is found in adjustment.* Unquestionably, life is subject to the variable winds that blow from every direction. They are not always at our back. And certainly we cannot change the wind, but we can adjust the sails to every wind that blows. Therein is a necessary condition to the solution of life's problems. It is either adjust or be miserable, or even be broken.

We recently had a storm in Fort Worth that did considerable damage. I observed two large trees near my home that were broken off and leveled. Not being able to adjust and bend, the trees were destroyed. Other trees, more flexible and more adjusting, came through the storm without harm. Obviously, there is more protection in flexibility than in bigness.

Life is like this. Either adjust to the circumstances or be battered and left with the pain of misery. However, rather than adjust, many people only wish to be otherwise than they are, to live in the fanciful circumstances they choose rather than in the real conditions that exist. "If only I could be placed in another setting, how much happier I would be!" "Oh, that I had…" These are the disquieting words of the troubled malcontents. But a change of settings will change only the place, not the person; and *where* one is, is not as important as *what* he is.

As an example, there is a plant in Palestine known as the Rose of Jericho, which flourishes under the most diverse and adverse circumstances: in the hot desert, in the rocky crevices, by the dusty wayside, in the rubbish heap. Even more amazing, the fierce, hot, dust-laden winds that blow from the African deserts will sometimes tear it from its place and fling it far out to sea, and there, driven by the storm and tossed by the salt waves, it still lives and grows. How does it manage to do it? Acceptance. Adjustment. It accepts and adjusts to the circumstances under which it must live.

◆ *For us, it is in and through the Holy Trinity* that the demanding adjustments are easier to make. Our trust in God gives us strength to hold up and find help, though battered from every side, as the Psalmist stated:

*The Lord is my strength and my shield;*
*my heart trusted in him, and I am helped;*
*therefore my heart greatly rejoiceth;*
*and with my song will I praise him.*
—PSALM 28:7

Assured of God's presence, we have the hopefulness to make the needed arrangements to meet the changing circumstances of life, and thereby find joy. Again we quote the Psalmist:

*Thou wilt show me the path of life:*
*in thy presence is fulness of joy;*
*at thy right hand there are pleasures for evermore.*
—PSALM 16:11

In the Lord's word, due to our belief in it and obedience to it, adjustments come naturally and so does joy. Without it, no one can experience the fullest internal peace. Hear Jesus on this subject:

*These things have I spoken unto you,*
*that my joy might remain in you,*
*and that your joy might be full.*
—JOHN 15:11

Life is still what you make it. You are the secret to happiness, not circumstances.

Of course, in every life some troubles must come, some storms must strike. But brave and believing, fortified and adjusted to meet whatever occurs, we know that following the blasts of a stormy night the quiet of a peaceful morn shall dawn.

> *Weeping may endure for a night,*
> *but joy cometh in the morning.*
> —PSALM 30:5

◆ *Another factor in making adjustments is for one to think and live outside himself.* "Look not every man on his own things but every man also on the things of others" (Philippians 2:4). This calls for a big, unselfish heart. Indeed, selfishness becomes the prison for a person's own soul.

> *Oh, doom beyond the saddest guess,*
> *As the long years of God unroll,*
> *To make thy dreary selfishness*
> *The prison of a soul.*
> —JOHN GREENLEAF WHITTIER

Getting out of self will take the emptiness out of your life and fill it with joy.

◆ *It is in losing yourself that you actually find yourself—and happiness.* Nineteen hundred years ago Jesus laid down this principle for the abundant and enjoyable life: "He that findeth his life shall lose it, and he that loseth his life for my sake shall find it" (Matthew 10:39).

You can find a new life of delightful satisfaction in losing yourself. This is evidenced by your enjoyment of a game—by losing yourself in the game, you are thrilled. True of music—only by forgetting yourself can you find it enrapturing. This is also a bona fide fact of employment—by putting yourself into your work it becomes pleasant and satisfying. Likewise, you have to go out to your friends to enjoy their friendship.

This point I emphasized to a lady, as well as to many others, who came to me with these words: "I'm not awfully miserable, but I'm not as happy as I should be. Can you help me?"

"Well, helping people is my stock in trade; let's see," was my immediate reply. Then I handed her a piece of paper and a pencil and said, "I want you to think of the unhappiest, most maladjusted person you know. Now I want you to make a list of the traits that describe that person."

This is the list she made: "1. Thinks the world revolves around her. 2. What she does for others is for her sake and not theirs. 3. Self-conscious. 4. Touchy. 5. Spiteful. 6. Unforgiving. 7. Unfair. 8. Envious. 9. Shirks duties. 10. Gossipy. 11. Divisive. 12. Hateful. 13. Critical of others. 14. Wishes to be appreciated without doing that which commends appreciation and to be loved without loving."

As I looked over her list, I commented: "Not a very pretty picture. No wonder she's miserable. Of course, this is an extreme case, the unhappiest person you know, but it does give us a lot of diagnostic facts. *She is unhappy because of the person she is.* So in order to achieve the fullest life into which the most sunshine pours, develop and cultivate the opposite traits of that poor woman. Make a list of the opposites. Meditate on them. Cultivate them, and more peace and joy will fill your heart and radiate your life."

This is sure to work because an irrevocable law is: "For whatsoever a man soweth, that shall he also reap" (Galatians 6:7).

### THE BEST WILL COME BACK TO YOU

*Give love, and love to your heart will flow,*
  *A strength in your utmost need;*
*Have faith, and a score of hearts will show*
  *Their faith in your word and deed.*

*For life is the mirror of king and slave,*
  *'Tis just what you are and do;*
*Then give to the world the best you have*
  *And the best will come back to you.*
—MADELINE BRIDGE

◆ *In keeping with the thesis that joy is attained by being somebody rather than by seeking it,* Jesus gave the celebrated Beatitudes in the immortal Sermon on the Mount. The Latin word *beatitudo*, from which our English word *beatitude* is derived, denotes blessedness, bliss, happiness. Thus, the Beatitudes in the King James Bible begin with the word "blessed," and in keeping with the same truth some other translations begin with the word "happy."

A Bible school teacher was reviewing his teenage class on the previous week's lesson on the Beatitudes. One girl, not well acquainted with the Bible, was asked what was last week's lesson. She replied, "the Be-happys." Really, that is about the best name for them.

> *Happy are the poor in spirit:*
> *for theirs is the kingdom of heaven.*
> *Happy are they that mourn:*
> *for they shall be comforted.*
> *Happy are the meek:*
> *for they shall inherit the earth.*
> *Happy are they which do hunger and thirst after*
> *righteousness: for they shall be filled.*
> *Happy are the merciful: for they shall obtain mercy.*
> *Happy are the pure in heart: for they shall see God.*

*Happy are the peacemakers:*
*for they shall be called the children of God.*
*Happy are they which are persecuted for righteous-*
*ness' sake: for theirs is the kingdom of heaven.*
—MATTHEW 5:3-10

The principles in the Beatitudes tell us how to live, and happiness becomes the by-product of a lofty life. You do not chase happiness, if you wish to find it. Instead, you just do right. For happiness has a way of fleeing from the person who seeks it; but to the person who becomes what the Spirit wants one to be, joy just naturally comes.

This joy—happiness—that comes from the highest quality of living, effected by our association with God, is more than a surface-only pleasantness. It is deeper than that. With this kind of joy which is a fruit of the Spirit we do not have to try to smile and to be happy. It just naturally manifests itself. It is not like the forced smiles of the man who ran for sheriff. When the votes were counted and he had lost, his comment was, "I'm glad it's over, because my face was getting so tired of smiling."

◆ *To refuse, however, to meet the conditions where-by you naturally become a joyful person is but to invite unhappiness*, as Solomon stated:

*Remember now thy Creator in the days of thy youth, while the evil days come not, nor the years draw nigh, when thou shalt say, I have no pleasure in them.*

—ECCLESIASTES 12:1

This trust and remembrance of the divine One, and all that is implied with it, lets you live each day in the most satisfying manner, meeting each day's problems as they come, as best as you can. After all, the best preparation for tomorrow is to fully live today, taking care of today}s responsibilities. "Sufficient unto the day is the evil thereof" (Matthew 6:34). This is the only way life can be lived—one day at a time, not in the lump. This gives you today.

*Happy the man, and happy he alone,*
  *He who can call today his own;*
  *He who, secure within, can say,*
*Tomorrow, do thy worst, for I have lived today.*
—JOHN DRYDEN

◆ *Furthermore, joy will enhance health and add days to this life.* Our attitudes affect our health. Many of the bodily ills are emotionally caused. In keeping with this fact, long before modern science ever coined the expression, *psychosomatic medicine*, Solomon stated, "A merry heart doeth good like a medicine" (Proverbs

17:22). Solomon was right, and so was John Wolcot
who said:

*Care to our coffin adds a nail, no doubt;*
*And every grin so merry, draws one out.*

*You have brought me so much joy in my life. Thank you.*

GARDENS OF THE HEART

PEACE

GARDENS OF THE HEART

Peace—a fruit of the Spirit. But, which peace is it? The internal peace within oneself? Or the external peace that one maintains with others? Perhaps no one can say with absolute certainty.

# 3 "PEACE"

Either way the results are the same. If it be an inward peace with God and self, it is sure to produce an outward peace among men, if it is possible (Romans 12:18). On the other hand, if it is an outside peace with associates, this is achieved only by first attaining peace within ourselves. For it is from within the individual that fightings and wars come (James 4:1); and likewise it is from within a person that community peace comes. A cause and effect relationship. This is why they are hard to separate.

♦ *Surely, the teachings of the Spirit produce within a person a personal peace with God and self.* For example:

1) Obedience to the Spirit's commandments provides the "answer of a good conscience toward God" (I Peter 3:21) which gives inner peace.

2) Also, faith in the Spirit's promises is sure to calm and quiet man within; promises like, "Seek ye first the kingdom of God, and his righteousness; and all these things (material needs) shall be added unto you" (Matthew 6:33), and "...lo, I am with you alway, even unto the end of the world" (Matthew 28:20), and "...this is the promise that he hath promised us, even eternal life" (I John 2:25).

Fortified with the peace of heart that comes from divine assurances, one reacts with positiveness and optimism, as follows:

> *We are troubled on every side,*
>   *yet not distressed;*
> *We are perplexed,*
>   *but not in despair;*
> *Persecuted, but not forsaken;*
> *Cast down, but not destroyed.*
> —II CORINTHIANS 4:8,9

But probably the specific peace that Paul listed

as a fruit of the Spirit is peace with people, the harmonious life with others. Paul had just stated that a work of the flesh is "strife...factions, divisions" (American Standard Version), and now the reader would expect Paul in giving the fruit of the Spirit to contrast it with the works of the flesh and that the "peace" mentioned is the outward peace that is opposed to outward strife. And definitely, it is sure to be achieved, if possible, as a natural consequence of or relationship to Divinity. For—

*When a man's ways please the Lord, he maketh*
*even his enemies to be at peace with him.*
—PSALM 34:14

So now let us think on this kind of *peace that reaches out to others*, which emanates from a mature and peaceable disposition. This peace is found in the good-natured temperament that pursues the ideals and principles that produce it.

◆ *One of which is forbearance.* The Bible teaches this beautiful and clement, human and merciful disposition: "With all lowliness and meekness, with long-suffering, forbearing one another in love" (Ephesians 4:2). Forbearance is an additive to peace within one's heart and thus within society. Remember that all temperaments are not the same, nor all the circumstances which surround people parallel. It is easy to say, "If I were So-and-so, I would do this or that." But if you were in that one's place, you might not know what to do—it is easy to talk.

It is to our advantage to make allowances for culture and circumstances, temper and training. Personal backgrounds are grounds for the more magnanimous spirit. Remember—many people have a self under surface that makes them better than you think; and under right influence those hidden qualities can be brought outside. This view will adorn your personality with patience, congeniality and loveliness.

If you could only witness the terrible struggles passing in the heart of that one whose vivacity annoys you...if you could see the tears that are shed in secret, the vexation felt, you would indeed show pity. Love that person! Make allowances!

◆ *Furthermore, in the pursuit of peace, go the second mile.* The Prince of Peace said, "And whosoever shall compel thee to go a mile, go with him twain" (Matthew 5:41).

Going the second mile requires unselfishness. I think the one thing that interferes with peaceful associations more than anything else is selfishness.

> *Real glory springs from the silent conquest*
> *of ourselves;*

*And without this, the conqueror is naught*
*but the first slave.*

Going the second mile also demands meekness. The abundant and the delightful life of peace within yourself, which is the first prerequisite of peace with others, is promised to the meek. The Psalmist said:

*But the meek shall inherit the earth; and shall*
*delight themselves in the abundance of peace.*
—PSALM 37:11

Meekness is gentle, longsuffering and humble. It is not domineering, blustering or arrogant.

One of the main causes of strife is pride. The Bible says, "He that is of a proud heart stirreth up strife" (Proverbs 28:2). When you get to the origin of strife in a school, club, church or business, the chances are you will find wounded pride. Someone feels by-passed, overlooked, unacknowledged or unappreciated. Egotism has been deflated.

A Sunday school teacher who felt that she had been by-passed in the teaching program began to fret and spew, and then resent and attack. The cause of her negative and miserable behavior was wounded pride. Its despicable conquests of blighted hearts and broken friendships run into the millions. What an enemy of man!

The distance from where you are to peace is more than a step—at least, a second mile. Whatever you have to do to trek the journey, do it; and you will be repaid a thousandfold.

◆ *Likewise, peace with your associates* is found in passing over another's transgression. The Bible says:

> *The discretion of a man deferreth his anger; and it is his glory to pass over a transgression.*
> —PROVERBS 19:11

There is glory in passing over another's infraction. Let it rest! Ah! How many hearts on the brink of misgiving and turmoil have been made serene and happy by this simple suggestion.

Some proceeding has wounded you by its want of tact; let it pass; no one will think of it again.

A censorious or unjust sentence irritates you; let it go; he who gave vent to it will be pleased to see it is forgotten.

A galling rumor has the splitting and tortuous force to estrange you from an old friend; let it rest, and thus preserve your charity and peace of mind. Ten chances to one, it is not true anyway.

A suspicious look is on the point of cooling your affection; let it rest, and your own look of trust will restore that one's confidence. Life is so much sweeter when we pass over the bitter experiences.

◆ *Additionally, to have peace we must be forgiving.* In the Lord's Prayer of example we are taught to pray:

> *And forgive us our debts, as we forgive our debtors.*
> —MATTHEW 6:12

If you cannot forgive, you obstruct the road over which you yourself must travel. For all have erred.

Neither can you have peace with others unless you forgive; because, sooner or later, you will feel that you have been wronged. Then there is the trouble which stirs within you and later breaks out of you into strife. But he who forgives ends the quarrel; then he finds calmness and concord, peace and pleasantness.

◆ *The submissive, yielding disposition*—in contrast with the obstinate, stubborn spirit—is essential to peaceable relationships. "Not selfwilled" (Titus 1:7) is one of the qualifications of a bishop or elder who occupies the role of an example to the flock. And those to the contrary who walk after the flesh are presumptuous and self-willed (II Peter 2:10).

Even common sense tells us that the give-and-take spirit is more profitable than unmovable stubbornness. This is seen in the fable of two goats that met on a log that stretched over a stream. This presented a problem because neither wanted to go back. A hard-headed approach could destroy both. So, instead of butting heads, they got their heads together in a wise solution. It was decided that one would lie down and let the other walk over him to safety, and then the goat lying down could arise and pursue his journey without danger. It was the agreeable, submissive spirit that saved them from harm.

◆ *Here are three additional directives for peace* in one verse in the Bible—so much said in so few words:

> *And that ye study to be quiet, and to do your own business, and to work with your own hands, as we commanded you.*
> —I THESSALONIANS 4:11

1) Quietness and peace go together. "A quiet and peaceable life" (I Timothy 2:2). The quiet person is able to work out human differences and attain peaceful solutions, while the noisy person only waves red flags and throws fat on the fire.

2) Minding your own business—not the other fellow's—is an excellent rule for staying out of trouble. All of us have enough to do just to look after our own business without meddling and probing in other people's business. "But let none of you suffer as a...busy-

body in other men's matters" (I Peter 4:15). This is good religion. Practical. Relevant. It rebukes the eavesdroppers, nosy pryers, skeleton diggers, gossipers, and know-it-alls who hasten to give advice that is not asked.

3) Work—a little word with big rewards no matter which way you look at it. Work to have (Ephesians 4:28). Furthermore, by working, you save yourself from an idleness that often opens the door to dissension. Doing nothing is ungratifying and unsettling which often finds its outlet in picking a fuss with somebody else. Truly, "idleness is the devil's workshop," and one of his works is strife-making. There is much personal protection in being so busy making a living, looking after your own business, doing good to others, that you do not have time to fuss and fight.

◆ *Summed up*, we see from the foregoing that to have peace we must "follow after the things which make for peace" (Romans 14:19). Peace is something we attain on purpose. It does not occur accidentally. Thus there is wisdom in the command: "Seek peace, and pursue it" (Psalm 34:14).

GARDENS OF THE HEART

LONGSUFFERING

LONGSUFFERING

GARDENS OF THE HEART

If we lived the life of a hermit, hidden and protected from a world of imperfect people that err in their judgments of us and in their dealings with us, there would be no need to be longsuffering.

# 4 LONGSUFFERING

But most of us are not isolated from the world. Neither do we want to be. We like to be with people, even though they sometimes hurt us. But the injury is much easier to bear if we are patient. For after all, the intensity and severity of a hurt is more in the mind of the sufferer than in the act itself. This is why the same hurt affects people in different ways. It may drive one person to have a nervous breakdown, while the other grins, bears it and throws it off.

So let us be practical. Our society is fallible. Our associates err. The members of our family make mistakes. All are human. Therefore, longsuffering is a *must* for the whole human family. We need it for a workable relationship with others. And we need it to preserve our own peace of mind and tranquility. I like what Jean Baptiste Poquelin said more than three hundred years ago:

> *If everyone were clothed with integrity, if every heart were just, frank, kindly, the other virtues would be well-nigh useless, since their chief purpose is to make us bear with patience the injustice of our fellows.*

♦ *Longsuffering protects mankind from self-destruction.* Men, therefore, must not turn themselves into brutish savages that kill themselves by gnashing one another, yet let us face facts. I sometimes think that the church is the only army that destroys its own wounded. It is so contradictory of our own profession. Outrageous. Shocking. Why can we not learn? For both human experience and Scripture teach that this is self-destruction, because it lays waste to both the destroyed and the destroyer.

> *If ye bite and devour one another, take heed that ye be not consumed one of another.*
> —GALATIANS 5:15

♦ *This beautiful quality—longsuffering—is not what some people think it is.* Patient endurance of injury is not cowardice or a lack of metal. For it requires more courage to be patient than it does to attack.

Neither is it a lack of energy or enthusiasm.

It is a recognition of human weakness from which no person is totally exempt, and a tolerance that puts the best interpretation on things.

It is one of the graces of love: "Love suffereth long" (I Corinthians 13:4). Hate hastens the condemnation of a wrong that is suffered, but love tempers it with patience.

◆ *The spirit of patient forbearance is a basic quality essential to the development of other beautiful traits* that go into the makeup of the most lovely personalities. Only the patient-under-injury person is prepared to obey this command:

> *Love your enemies, bless them that curse you, do good to them that hate you, and pray for them which despitefully use you, and persecute you.*
> —MATTHEW 5:44

◆ *Understandably, it is only the longsufferer* who is qualified to turn the other cheek:

> *But whosoever shall smite thee on thy right cheek, turn to him the other also.*
> —MATTHEW 5:39

◆ *Furthermore, it is the longsufferer rather than*

*the short-fused person* who is prepared to abide by this Scripture:

> *Let every man be swift to hear,*
> *slow to speak, slow to wrath.*
> —JAMES 1:19

Many, many people who are out of tune with this verse are not bullies, but there is one thing sure: the bully is exceedingly impatient. The big bully with the little brain. Maybe his bullyness developed in a futile effort to compensate for his inferior mentality. The only way he knows to handle his wishes and problems is to be a browbeater. Others must submit or suffer his wrath. No unselfish consideration. No real chivalry. True, he has drive but so does the brute.

♦ *Another helpful thing longsuffering has going for it is time.* Time is on its side. It gives more time for problems to solve themselves. Most of them would go away if left alone. Patience ordinarily achieves more than force. It is better to delay than to err, so give time a chance. Of course, this requires level-headedness and sterling character, for longsuffering may mean self-suffering, personal endurance of injury, free of anger and vexation.

♦ *The Bible holds up the prophets as examples of suffering affliction and of patience*, and Job's name is mentioned in particular (James 5:10,11). Poor Job—after his abundant properties had been wiped out, after his sons and daughters had been struck down in death, after his own body had been afflicted with boils from head to toe, after his own wife failed him in the time of need and advised him to "curse God and die," his patient endurance carried him through. Rather than give up, he bravely uttered these heroic and immortal words: "Though he slay me, yet will I serve him." With that kind of patience and grit, we are not surprised to learn that later he was blessed twofold over all he had lost.

So in times of affliction and stress, when our metal is being tested, let us never lose faith in God's care for us and ability to lift our burdens. The thing is—His timing may be just a little different from ours. While the relief may not come as soon as we wish, it is to our advantage when "patience have her perfect work, that ye may be perfect and entire, wanting noth-ing" (James 1:4).

◆ *It is true that patience is sometimes difficult* but its fruit is always sweet. Numerous examples could be given. This one I especially like:

An employee of a few weeks was the brunt of many unkind jokes and nasty slurs, yet he kept his cool and suffered in silence. His demeanor was always mild, kind and non-retaliatory. The most common criticism of some of the office force centered around his beard. One day he was asked, "Do you think that beard looks good on you?" He replied, "No, I certainly don't, but I think I look better with it than I do without it." Then he parted the beard at a place and said, "You see that scar? This beard hides that scar. I got that scar in World War II. I'm not complaining, for I'm very lucky to be alive. If that enemy soldier had been a tiny bit closer with that bayonet, he would have cut my head off."

Now their mockery turned into admiration. How ashamed they were. This would not have resulted, however, if he had built up bitterness beforehand.

◆ *Truly, the blessings of patience are unlimited.* What it can do for our society staggers our conception. In the words of Bishop Horne, it is "the preserver of peace, the cherisher of love, the teacher of humility. Patience strengthens the spirit, sweetens the temper, stifles anger, extinguishes envy, subdues pride: she bridles the tongue, restrains the hand, tramples upon temptations, endures persecutions. Patience produces unity in the church, loyalty in the state, harmony in families and societies; she comforts the poor, and moderates the rich; she makes us humble in prosperity, cheerful in adversity, unmoved by calumny and reproach; she teaches us to forgive those who have injured us, and to be the first in asking forgiveness of those whom we have injured; she delights the faithful, and invites the unbelieving; she adorns the woman, and approves the man; she is beautiful in either sex and in every age.

"Behold her appearance and her attire! Her countenance is calm and serene as the face of heaven unspotted by the shadow of a cloud; and no wrinkle of grief or anger is seen in her forehead. Her eyes are as the eyes of doves for meekness, and on her eyebrows sit cheerfulness and joy. Her mouth is lovely in silence; her complexion and color that of innocence and security. She is clothed in the robes of the martyrs, and in her hand she holds a scepter in the form of a cross. She rides not in the whirlwind and stormy tempest of passion, but her throne is the humble and contrite heart, and her kingdom is the kingdom of peace."

◆ *Summed up*, longsuffering—steadfast patience—gives one power to possess his soul. After Jesus told his disciples that they would be hated of all men for His name's sake and promised them that they would not be harmed, then He said:

> *In your patience possess ye your souls.*
> —LUKE 21:19

GARDENS OF THE HEART

KINDNESS

Kindness is gentle, and gentleness is kind. Hence, one translation of the Scriptures uses the word gentleness, while another renders it kindness. As you know, it is a fruit of the Spirit.

# 5 KINDNESS

Furthermore, it is a mark of the highest person. Nevertheless, many of the world have falsely held the view that a rough and tough disposition is preferable. But roughshod manners never triumph for long, for sooner or later rudeness encounters rudeness, roughness meets roughness, and the eruption that follows leaves neither a winner. If you cannot win by being a gentle lady or a kind gentleman, then the winning is not worth your stooping beneath yourself which would be no victory at all. This is the more excellent and kingly way:

> *And the servant of the Lord must not strive; but be gentle unto all men...patient.*
> —II TIMOTHY 2:24

*But we were gentle among you, even as a nurse*
*cherisheth her children.*
—I THESSALONIANS 2:7

*But the wisdom that is from above is first pure,*
*then peaceable, gentle, and easy to be entreated,*
*full of mercy and good fruits, without partiality,*
*and without hypocrisy.*
—JAMES 3:17

Indeed, there is no effectiveness in human rela-
tions—public or private—that is greater than simple
kindness.

◆ *Gentleness or kindness is a gracious quality ever*
*needed in our society.*

*So many paths that wind and wind;*
*When just the art of being kind*
*Is all this sad world needs.*
—ELLA WHEELER WILCOX

◆ *This sweetness of disposition is opposed* to a
harsh, barbarous, rude temperament that causes trouble and promotes unhappiness. Our world is hard
enough without the ruffles caused by the sour,
crabbed, unkind individual; it has enough troubles
exclusive of the commotions created by the cold, cruel
person. A little kindness makes a big difference, and
gives much joy to everybody.

*A kind heart is a fountain of gladness, making everything in its vicinity freshen into smiles.*
—WASHINGTON IRVING

◆ *It is truly a delight to be with the mild, calm, benign person;* and inasmuch as like begets like, the same spirit rubs off on others. Indeed, kind associates are what we all need. Give me the considerate look! The gentle voice! The kind hand! I need it. Furthermore, I respond more graciously to good treatment. And, generally speaking, so does the other fellow. And as my path crosses his and my words meet his, may I keep this in mind and treat him respectfully and kindly. He is apt to pass it on, at least a little of it. And that is what the world needs.

> *Have you had a kindness shown?*
>   *Pass it on.*
> *It was not given to you alone,*
>   *Pass it on.*
> *Let it travel through the years;*
> *Let it wipe another's tears;*
> *Till in heaven the deed appears,*
>   *Pass it on.*

◆ *Now let us search our souls:* If we are never kind to others what good are we in the world? None! No good to self, no good to one's fellowman. Life is only a vain existence. However—

> *If by one word I help another,*
> *A struggling and despairing brother,*
>   *Or ease one bed of pain;*
> *If I but aid some sad one weeping,*
> *Or comfort one, lone vigil keeping,*
>   *I have not lived in vain.*

Moreover, the unkind life is more than vain; it is waste, wasted living. For that person misses the happiest and more profitable part of living. The gentle acts of kindness and love will live on forever—in another life and maybe on another shore.

### KINDNESS LIVES FOREVER

> *Kind words can never die;*
>   *Cherished and blest,*
> *God knows how deep they lie*
>   *Stored in the breast,*
> *Like childhood's simple rhymes,*
> *Said o'er a thousand times*
> *Aye, in all lands and climes*
>   *Distant and near.*

> *Sweet thoughts can never die,*
>   *Though, like the flowers,*
> *Their brightest hues may fly*
>   *In wintry hours;*

*But when the gentle dew*
*Gives them their charm anew,*
*With many an added hue*
　*They bloom again.*
—AUTHOR UNKNOWN

◆ *Kindness is a pleasing and powerful sermon in practice*—one nobody misunderstands. Even the deaf can hear and the blind can see kindness. The Four Gospels we commonly speak of are Matthew, Mark, Luke and John, and the fifth is kindness. Those who never read nor hear the four can be swayed by the fifth, for it is very visible and exceedingly audible. It unmistakably comes through clearly and persuasively. This we see from Peter's exposition of the topic:

> *If any obey not the word, they (husbands) also may without the word be won by the conversation (conduct) of their wives.*
> —I PETER 3:1

During the Korean War a chaplain saw a severely wounded soldier lying on the field of battle. Wanting to minister to him, he inquired, "Would you like for me to read some strengthening passages from the Bible?"

"Right now I had rather have a drink. I'm dying of thirst," was the reply.

And away rushed the chaplain who soon returned with water to quench the fallen soldier's thirst. Then he took off his scarf, rolled it into a little pillow, and placed it under the soldier's head.

"I'm so cold," mumbled the badly wounded soldier.

On hearing this, the chaplain removed his top coat and spread it over the ill man.

"Now," whispered the attended soldier, "if there's anything in that book that makes you so kind, read it to me, please."

As seen in this forceful example, it is the Fifth Gospel—kindness—that often opens the door of the heart to the entrance of the first four.

A pioneer preacher asked for a lighted candle. But the flame went out because the maid hurried too fast before it reached its full strength. It was then that the discerning minister made an application. He said, "Let this be a lesson for us in dealing with weaker people. If the candle when first lighted had been carried slowly and shielded by the hand from the air, it would have burned with vigor instead of going out. In like manner, many a weak, dimmed person might be put to shining, if we approached him gently with a helping hand."

◆ *It is obvious that an urgent need* in this world of ours that has turned insensitive to the wants of others is to *show a heart*. For it takes a heart to win a heart. I am inclined to believe what Henry Ward Beecher said: "Though the world needs reproof and correction, it needs kindness more; though it needs the grasp of the strong hand, it needs, too, the open palm of love and tenderness."

◆ *Maybe some of our unkindness is due to a failure to think.* I am not trying to excuse any of us, just trying to be realistic and fair, but *maybe some of our unkindness is due to a failure to think*. "I wasn't thinking" is an often belated explanation of our rough manners. The hurt, nevertheless, was done and a heart was wounded.

> *The wounds I might have healed,*
>   *The human sorrow and smart!*
> *And yet it never was in my soul*
>   *To play so ill a part.*
> *But evil is wrought by want of thought*
>   *As well as want of heart.*
> —THOMAS HOOD

So let's be thoughtful. We are dealing with sensitive human beings. Be kind! Be kind! Remember—

everyone you meet is bearing a heavy burden and fighting a hard battle, and many of them with a weak back and a short stick.

*And be ye kind one to another.*
—EPHESIANS 4:32

◆ *Moreover, Jesus looks upon kindness to others as acts of gentleness to Himself.* He said, "Inasmuch as ye have done it unto one of the least of these my brethren, ye have done it unto me" (Matthew 25:40). Many of us think we would have been glad to have been with Jesus when He lived in the flesh on earth, and to have ministered to His needs: to provide shelter, to prepare meals, to furnish clothing, and to accompany Him on His daily ministries. That we cannot do, for the timing is wrong. But we can, according to His own word, still minister to Him by feeding the hungry, by giving drink to the thirsty, by providing shelter for the stranger, by supplying clothing for the needy, and by visiting the persecuted and the outcasts (Matthew 25:35-40).

Hence, according to the accounting of Jesus, the time to minister to Him is ever opportune. It is achieved in the area of human kindness. Now it is up to us.

Who in our community needs a meal? Who needs a place to live and a few simple clothes for their children? The homeless, the helpless, the hopeless of our society are waiting.

You ask about rewards? As we begin to reach out to them, we should see in each one of them the face of our Lord Jesus. Is that not reward enough?

# 6  GOODNESS

The good heart from which the good deeds come is essential. "For out of it are the issues of life" (Proverbs 4:23). No mistake about it. Pure water can flow only from a pure spring; and, likewise, goodness can emanate only from "the honest and good heart" (Luke 8:15).

Just as good fruit is the yield of a good tree, so is goodness the product of a good person. What might otherwise seem to be goodness is only superficial, self-serving and short-lived. Furthermore, the most accurate test of a good person is the fruit he bears:

> *Ye shall know them by their fruits...Even so every good tree bringeth forth good fruit;*

*but a corrupt tree bringeth forth evil fruit.*
—MATTHEW 7:16,17

◆ *Goodness—it is an excellence God has in all its completeness and perfection,* so much of it that He cannot sin. Such goodness staggers the imagination. While Jesus was living in the flesh, He was subject to flesh's temptations and thus could have sinned—could have but did not; and while living in this state He described God with an exclusive goodness, saying, "Why callest thou me good? none is good, save one, that is, God" (Luke 18:19). Hence, goodness in its fullest degree and in its most perfect state is a word used to describe only God. Therefore, the conclusion is clear: The more of God a person has in him, the more goodness he possesses.

◆ *Goodness is the very thing Jesus went about doing:*

> *Who went about doing good…*
> *for God was with him.*
> —ACTS 10:38

Actual goodness. No showmanship. Not an appeal to the grandstands. It was natural goodness, just as natural as it is for the rivers to flow. It was natural for Jesus to do good because He was good; and He was good, as the verse says, because "God was with him." That was the source and impetus of His goodness.

Accordingly, the followers of Divinity also do good because they are good; and they are made good because of their association with God. One of the grandest and most significant compliments ever paid man is his being called good. It was said of Barnabas:

> *For he was a good man.*
> —ACTS 11:24

He was a man—no angel—frail man made of the same clay common to all of us; but he was so improved and matured in goodness that his name has been handed down through the ages in commendation. Enrolled and made famous in the Scriptures. Evidently he had become a good man by winning battles over evil. What he became—goodness—is a fruit of the Spirit and he achieved it by walking in the Spirit. "Walk in the Spirit, and ye shall not fulfill the lust of the flesh"—do evil (Galatians 5:16).

◆ *Yes definitely, there is power in goodness to overcome evil.* This is the good person's way of overcoming wickedness. Correctly so, we are admonished to prevail in this manner. "Be not overcome of evil, but overcome evil with good" (Romans 12:21).

It works!

Some young girls called on an elderly lady who

had moved into their block. The gracious old lady spoke to them about going to church. In their disrespect of age and irreverence of religion, one of them insultingly said, "I don't see how that even God can love an ugly old woman like you."

The dear old lady replied, "Honey, that is one of the marvelous things about God. He can and does love an ugly old woman like me, wrinkled and stooped, thin and hollow-eyed, half crippled with arthritis, and not worth very much to anybody. Isn't it wonderful? Because He loves me, I love Him and you and everybody else."

It was then that the little girls began to cry.

Good had overcome evil.

◆ *Truly, goodness is the best of all human qualities in action:* thoughtfulness, truthfulness, sympathy, fairness, kindness, unselfishness, helpfulness, generosity, tolerance and forgiveness. It is yard work for the neighbor who is down in his back. It is house cleaning for the woman who has had surgery. It is medicine to the sick. Food to the hungry. Lenience to the bungler. Forgiveness to the offender. It is a lift to the fallen. A push to the discouraged, and a song to the hopeless. It is bigness to both friends and enemies, for goodness has no room for littleness. It is a heart, a big heart! To everybody! In our social and business lives it is the

Golden Rule in practice: the doing unto others as you would have them do unto you (Matthew 7:12).

◆ *Furthermore, the person filled with goodness just naturally abounds* "to every good work" (II Corinthians 9:8). He has the feeling that inclines Him to do as John Wesley said:

> *Do all the good you can,*
> *By all the means you can,*
> *In all the ways you can,*
> *In all the places you can,*
> *At all the times you can,*
> *To all the people you can,*
> *As long as ever you can.*

◆ *Indeed, goodness has what it takes to make the world better.* It has eyes—a vision that sees good in others and appreciates them; and when evil is there, it sees it only for the purpose of turning it into good. Never for the intent of making a self-righteous comparison.

It has ears—open ears that hear the penetrating cries of the needy and the mournful sobs of the brokenhearted.

It has a strong back upon which others can cast their burdens. "Bear ye one another's burdens," is the ancient message to those who would be good.

It has hands—helping hands that are stretched out to those who are struggling and grasping to stay afloat.

It has feet—beautiful feet that leave footprints on the sands of time, pointing to the betterment of mankind.

◆ *In being good to others you are actually being good to yourself,* for the conscience of well doing is appreciation of life. It adds interest, zest and self-appreciation to life. It is a preventive against getting down on yourself. Therefore, "support the weak...it is more blessed to give than to receive" (Acts 20:35).

◆ *As life nears the end,* it is comforting to know that you have lived in goodness and given yourself to the benefit of mankind.

When Sir Walter Scott lay dying, he called for his son-in-law and biographer, Lockhart, and said to him, "Lockhart, my dear sir, be a good man. Be virtuous, be religious, be a good man. Nothing else will give you any comfort when you come to lie here."

◆ *Summed up,* perhaps there is no deeper or broader expression of goodness than the sentiments expressed in this beautiful and relevant prayer, which we all need to pray.

*Lord,*
*Make me an instrument of thy peace.*
*Where there is hatred, let me sow love;*
*Where there is injury, pardon;*
*Where there is doubt, faith;*
*Where there is despair, hope;*
*Where there is darkness, light; and*
*Where there is sadness, joy.*

*O divine Master,*
*Grant that I may not so much*
*Seek to be consoled as to console;*
*To be understood as to understand;*
*To be loved as to love;*
*For it is in giving that we receive;*
*It is in pardoning that we are pardoned; and*
*It is in dying that we are born to eternal life.*
—FRANCIS OF ASSISI

FAITHFULNESS · FAITHFULNESS · FAITHFULNESS · FAITHFULNESS · FAITHFULNESS · FAITHFULNESS

FAITHFULNESS · FAITHFULNESS · FAITHFULNESS · FAITHFULNESS · FAITHFULNESS · FAITHFULNESS

When one's life is influenced and led by the Spirit of God, faithfulness is sure to ensue. True religion works within us and forms and shapes the ideal person which has to include fidelity and loyalty.

# 7 FAITHFULNESS

In following God, we follow Him who is completely and perfectly faithful. "Know therefore that the Lord thy God, he is God, the faithful God, which keepeth covenant and mercy with them that love him and keep his commandments to a thousand generations" (Deuteronomy 7:9). There is no fickleness about Him. He never vacillates. He is as steady as the stars in the heaven, and why not? For He put them there. He is "the father of lights, with whom is no variableness, neither shadow of turning" (James 1:17). He is always the same, unchanging in the changing seasons, unmovable in the moving ages. There is no alteration in His being, His designs and His plans. What He was before the world began, He is now; and what He is now, he will be when the world is no more. Be sure of this: whatever changes may transpire in human circumstances, whatever adversities we may suffer, whatever deserts we have to traverse, whatever oceans we have to swim, whatever mountains we have to climb, and in whatever domain we may later dwell, God is the same.

◆ *It is refreshing and vitalizing, therefore, to know that God can be counted on.* We weak mortals, subject to flesh's temptations, sometimes slip and fall, but it is reassuring to know that the God who loves us never wavers.

> *It fortifies my soul to know*
> *That, though I perish, Truth is so:*
> *Whate'er I do, Thou dost not change.*
> *I steadier step when I recall*
> *That, if I slip, Thou dost not fall.*
> —ARTHUR HUGH CLOUGH

◆ *As we see, faithfulness is godlike and one of the most kingly traits.* It is character at its best. Something deep-seated and ingrained. After all, this is where God works, on the inside of man. "It is the same God which worketh all in all" (I Corinthians 12:6); and thereby we become somebody real and dependable, not superficial shells. We are not like the doughnuts where all the sugar is on the outside. Our true worth is in being genuine, not in feigned appearance:

> *True worth is in being, not seeming,*
>   *In doing, each day that goes by,*
> *Little duties, not in dreaming,*
>   *Of great things to do by and by.*
>
> *For whatever men say in their blindness,*
>   *And spite of the fancies of youth,*
> *Nothing is so kingly as faithfulness,*
>   *And nothing so royal as truth.*
> —ADAPTED, ALICE CARY

◆ *However, in all reality, constancy is not always easy and effortless.* Problems! Problems! Problems! We are harassed by trials, bled by sorrows, scourged by disappointments and assailed by losses. Any way you look at it, life is a struggle, and our pathway is marked with many pitfalls. Otherwise, we would not have been commanded to watch; there would have been no need for it. However, knowing man's needs, Jesus said, "Watch and pray, that ye enter not into temptation: the spirit indeed is willing, but the flesh is weak" (Matthew 26:41). But by looking beyond our own feebleness to God's might, trusting Him, we have born anew within us every day the spirit of fidelity. And thus we say,

> *I will not doubt though all my ships at sea*
> *Come drifting home with broken masts and sails,*
> *I will believe the Hand which never fails,*
> *From seeming evil worketh good for me;*
> *And though I weep because those sails are tattered,*
> *Still will I cry, while my best hope lies shattered,*
>   *"I trust in thee."*
> —ELLA WHEELER WILCOX

The faithful God still reigns; and "he maketh me to lie down in green pastures: he leadeth me beside the still waters. He restoreth my soul" (Psalm 23:2,3).

◆ *Trust in God makes us more faithful and trustworthy.* If not, religion has failed us, failed to make us what we ought to be; and true religion never miscarries: we may fail it, but it never fails us. With faith in God we find support and strength. As we meditate on this passage, faithfulness is rekindled within us:

> *I had fainted, unless I had believed to see*
> *the goodness of the Lord in the land of the living.*
> *Wait on the Lord: be of good courage, and he shall*
> *strengthen thine heart: wait, I say, on the Lord.*
> —PSALM 27:13,14

Wait on Him or serve Him, and you cannot fall short in your responsibilities to others.

◆ *Faithfulness is not necessarily excelling the other fellow;* rather it is doing the best you can with what you have. God does not expect us to perform a service to Him or others that we are not capable of performing. Faithfulness to our responsibilities includes only response to abilities, doing our best with our endowments and opportunities.

This is forcefully portrayed in the Parable of Talents (Matthew 25:14-30). A talent was a sum of money. We have the story in which a certain master called to him his servants and delivered to them his goods. To one he gave five talents, to another two, and to another one; to every man according to his several ability; and immediately took his journey. He that had received five talents went and traded and made five more. He that had been entrusted with two gained two more. But he that was given one was untrustworthy, went and digged in the earth and hid it.

After a long time the absent master returned and reckoned with his servants. To the servant who was given five and had gained five, he said, "Well done, thou good and faithful servant: thou hast been faithful over a few things, I will make thee ruler over many things: enter thou into the joy of thy lord" or master. It is marvelous and encouraging to us that the owner spoke the same message, word for word, to the

man who was given two and gained two. He had pro-
cured only forty per cent of what the five-talent man
had acquired, but the reward was exactly the same.
And for good reason because he had been just as faithful as the other.

It was the one who was handed the least—one
talent—that was faithless and untrue. This kindled the
anger of the master, and he called him a "wicked and
slothful servant." The conclusion is clear—unfaithful-
ness is wickedness. Nothing righteous about it.

This parable, simple and pointed, is irrefutable
evidence that the faithful Father requires us in our
faithfulness to do our best.

> *Like the star*
> *That shines afar*
> *Without haste*
> *And without rest*
> *Let each man wheel with steady sway*
> *Round the task that rules the day,*
> *And do his best!*

—JOHANN WOLFGANG VON GOETHE

♦ *All of us are stewards,* just like the men in the
Parable of Talents. Nothing is really ours. Everything
belongs to the Great Provider. He entrusts us for a
time with life, abilities and earthly benefits. We pass
but everything we thought we had remains, for it was

not ours. It was His. We are only the stewards, and stewards must be faithful. The Bible makes this plain: "Moreover it is required in stewards, that a man be found faithful" (I Corinthians 4:2).

Hence, no list of requirements for man is complete that does not include trustworthiness; neither is any catalog of beliefs entire that does not have it. Religion demands it. Family life requires it. Social life urges it. Business exacts it. So, in poetic truth, this we say:

*Faithfully faithful to every trust,*
*Honestly honest in every deed,*
*Righteously righteous and justly just;*
*This is the good man's practical creed.*

◆ *As expected, the Spirit-directed person is faithful* as a Christian, as a spouse, as a father or mother, as a son or daughter, as a friend, as a neighbor, and as a citizen. He or she is faithful in commitments made, in promises given, in words uttered, in debts contracted, and in duties enjoined. Any person who lacks such in his general behavior, accounting for the fact that all err at times, cannot very well claim to be a bearer of the fruit of the Spirit. "The tree is known by his fruit" (Matthew 12:33). And a fruit of the Spirit is faithfulness; thus if a person is not faithful, the Spirit has not been allowed to produce fruit in that life.

◆ *Now we call attention to some examples of this sterling quality:*

1) The allegiance of Moses the Hebrew is heartening. When he was an infant he was taken from a basket in the river by Pharaoh's daughter, was adopted by her and reared as an Egyptian royal prince. But later he turned his back upon the state riches and glories to lead his own people out of slavery. He chose "rather to suffer affliction with the people of God, than to enjoy the pleasures of sin for a season" (Hebrews 11:25).

And that was faithfulness—to his oppressed people and an unpopular cause.

2) Ruth's loyalty is a lovely and fascinating one. After her husband had died and after her father-in-law and another of his sons had died, it was then that her widowed mother-in-law Naomi, bereft of husband and two sons, planned to return to the land of Judah. Ruth wanted to accompany her mother-in-law; however, thinking of the young woman's future, Naomi insisted that she remain. In response, Ruth spoke these moving words of devotion, a real classic:

> *Entreat me not to leave thee, or to return from following after thee: for whither thou goest, I will go; and where thou lodgest, I will lodge: thy people shall be my people, and thy God my God.*
> —RUTH 1:16

And that was faithfulness—to a family need.

3) The constancy of Onesiphorus is impressive. Paul was a prisoner in Rome, not for any crime committed but for religious activities. Nero had struck terror in the hearts of many. But here was a man—Onesiphorus—who in the face of disfavor and danger did not desert Paul. And in deep appreciation, shortly before he was executed, Paul wrote: "The Lord give mercy unto the house of Onesiphorus: for he oft refreshed me, and was not ashamed of my chain. But, when he was in Rome, he sought me out very diligently, and found me" (II Timothy 1:16,17).

And that was faithfulness—to a Christian brother in time of trial.

4) The unfailing devotion of the early church is encouraging. During a great persecution they had to flee, but their devotion remained unchanged. "Therefore they that were scattered abroad went everywhere preaching the word" (Acts 8:4).

And that was faithfulness—to a cause.

*Let come what will, I mean to bear it out,*
*And either live with glorious victory*
*Or die with fame, renowned in chivalry.*
*He is not worthy of the honey-comb*
*That shuns the hive because the bees have stings.*
—WILLIAM SHAKESPEARE

5) Our renowned forefathers' allegiance to a political concept lifts our sometimes drooping spirits as we behold so much national good sacrificed for personal gain. It gave rise to a New Nation, a new bond in which they relied on Divine Providence and on one another. This was explicitly expressed in the Declaration of Independence:

> *And, for the support of the Declaration, with a firm reliance on the protection of Divine Providence, we mutually pledge to each other, our lives, our fortunes, and our sacred honor.*

And that was faithfulness—to national freedom, regardless of the struggles and sacrifices involved.

6) The Apostle Paul's uncompromising fidelity to the very end is inspiring. As a prisoner in Rome, soon to be led outside the gates of the city to be executed for his convictions, he penned among other things these dramatic words: "For I am now ready to be offered, and the time of my departure is at hand. I have fought a good fight, I have finished my course, I have kept the faith: henceforth there is laid up for me a crown of righteousness, which the Lord, the righteous judge, shall give me at that day" (II Timothy 4:6-8).

And that was faithfulness—to death.

The Lord said, "Be thou faithful unto death, and I will give thee a crown of life" (Revelation 2:10). Paul was.

Lastly, in the full analysis, faithfulness to self builds the bridge over which we pass to be true to other persons and causes.

> *This above all: to thine own self be true,*
> *And it must follow, as the night the day,*
> *Thou canst not then be false to any man.*
> —WILLIAM SHAKESPEARE

GARDENS OF THE HEART

MEEKNESS

> Jesus is the perfect example of lowli-
> ness and meekness. He said: "Come
> unto me, all ye that labor and are
> heavy laden, and I will give you rest.
> Take my yoke upon you, and learn of
> me; for I am meek and lowly in heart:
> and ye shall find rest unto your souls.
> For my yoke is easy, and my burden
> is light." —Matthew 11:28-30

# 8 MEEKNESS

"I am meek and lowly in heart." This was one of His sweet, endearing characteristics. No pomp. No false pretensions. No sudden anger. No lingering malice. No long-sought vengeance. Yet no person ever endured more wrongs or suffered them more patiently than He. Jesus was not oppressive, harsh and overbearing, not even in dealing with His enemies. He was the very opposite of a bully. The domineering are so artless, thoughtless, inconsiderate and destructive; despotic and tyrannical, they operate with about the same degree of breeding, tact and culture as a wild boar at a tea party. Jesus was the very antithesis of such a characterization. Nobody, nothing, not even the bloodthirsty men who hounded Him, ever broke the calmness of His life.

Jumping on the bandwagon of some passing fad or popular cause never concerned Him, for He never sought earthly recognition. Instead, He proclaimed, "My kingdom is not of this world." Although some thought evil of Him, it did not frustrate Him, for He had a calling and mission too big to allow little people and trivial circumstances to affect. Bad men's relentless efforts to lower His reputation did not ruffle Him, for He had already "made himself of no reputation" (Philippians 2:7). False accusations could not break His silence. "He answered nothing" (Matthew 27:12). "He was oppressed, and he was afflicted, yet he opened not his mouth: he was brought as a lamb to the slaughter, and as a sheep before her shearers is dumb, so he opened not his mouth" (Isaiah 53:7). "Who, when he was reviled, reviled not again; when he suffered, he threatened not; but committed himself to him that judgeth righteously" (I Peter 2:23). Jesus was willing to put all the wrongs He suffered in the hands of the Righteous Judge. Letting such matters rest with the Righteous Avenger brought Him internal peace. There was nothing the world could do to Him that could upset Him. For He was "meek and lowly in heart." Such a person is insulated and protected from the sources of man's restlessness—calculated calumny, hobbled hopes, punctured pride and shortsighted self-ishness.

Additionally, the Scripture says that we, too, achieve rest by learning of Him. "Learn of me," He says, "and ye shall find rest unto your souls." Thus rest is associated with learning. Not that we learn to rest; rather, we learn from Him a way of life that produces the peace within us. Soul rest, therefore, is not casual; it is causal. All nature proclaims that effects must have causes. Men do not "gather grapes of thorns, or figs of thistles" (Matthew 7:16). Our God is the God of law and order. The law of cause and effect is ever working. If we would have internal peace, the law says that we achieve it by learning of Jesus. By allowing ourselves to be directed by the Spirit's teachings, meekness will blossom and bear fruit in our lives. It will! Definitely it will! For meekness is one of the fruits or products of the Spirit. Then rest shall prevail in our souls. Many good things exist because of a circular, causal process. This is true of soul rest. The Spirit produces meek-ness, and meekness produces rest.

As meekness develops we become more like the Master who got down and washed the disciples' feet. His words still ring in our hearts: "If I then, your Lord and Master, have washed your feet; ye also ought to wash one another's feet. For I have given you an example, that ye should do as I have done to you" (John 13:14,15). No task, provided it is pure and honest, is beneath any person's doing.

> *Oh, why should the spirit of mortal be proud?*
> *Like a swift-flitting meteor, a fast-flying cloud,*
> *A flash of the lightning, a break of the wave,*
> *He passes from life to his rest in the grave.*
> —WILLIAM KNOX

◆ *Indeed, meekness is a personal ornamentation that is priceless in God's sight:*

> *Even the ornament of a meek and quiet spirit,*
> *which is in the sight of God of great price.*
> —I PETER 3:4

Meekness is of enormous value to Him whose values count the most. And what God treasures, man must not debase.

◆ *Meekness, however, is not what some people think it is.* Gross misunderstandings of its true meaning have cheapened and depreciated it.

It is not weakness; it is power. In speaking to

meek people, Paul said, "Bear ye one another's burdens, and so fulfill the law of Christ" (Galatians 6:2). This takes strength.

Neither is it bleakness; it is the way of joyfulness. The meek have much more fun than the overbearing.

Nor is it freakishness; it is the way of sanity. Bearing the fruit of the Spirit is not freakish. It makes good sense for one to have a refined disposition that is humble and submissive.

Nor is meekness cowardice or the surrender of one's rights. An outstanding example of this is Jesus who was "meek and lowly in heart" (Matthew 11:29). But He was not cowardly; instead, He was the bravest of the brave. Neither was He unconcerned about His rights, and He manifested this feeling in these words: "If I have done evil, bear witness of the evil; but if well, why smitest thou me?" (John 18:23). The Jesus who is spoken of as a lamb is also characterized as a lion: "lion of the tribe of Judah" (Revelation 5:5). In personal matters He behaved like a lamb, but when His teachings were attacked He arose with the fearlessness and combativeness of a lion.

Nevertheless, the world which is often wrong does not readily link meekness with courage. It prefers to take notice of the man who struts his bravery; it undersells the meek man's valor. Yet how often when bravery is tested, when the time comes to take a stand for principle and right, the lowly and unpretentious man astonishes everybody with his cool and unrelenting gallantry. It took grit for the early Christians to endure the persecutions they had to meet. Many of them died on crosses, on poles as burning torches, in pots of boiling oil, and in arenas as the helpless victims of lions. Meek but brave!

◆ *From the positive view*, meekness is patience and unpretentiousness in handling the affairs of life, especially injuries. It is too big to be easily offended. It never wears its feelings on its shoulders. It is not self-willed but is easily entreated. Never exalts itself. Knows no malice. Is never vengeful. It is a winsome quality for in its presence you are comfortable.

A missionary once asked some natives in a foreign land, "Who are the meek?" A little boy spoke up: "Those who turn the other cheek." Maybe not a full answer. Yet there is much truth in it.

◆ *The very basis for meekness is humility*. It understands man's place in the scheme of things: man's inferiority and God's superiority. Never tries to play God. It is a beautiful, childlike trait:

> *Whosoever therefore shall humble himself*
> *as this little child, the same is greatest*

*in the kingdom of heaven.*
—MATTHEW 18:4

*And whosoever shall exalt himself shall be abased; and he that shall humble himself shall be exalted.*
—MATTHEW 23:12

◆ *The most knowledgeable are usually the humblest and the meekest.* Origen, one of the wisest of all teachers, made this lowly admission: "This I know, that I know nothing." He continued, "I am not ignorant of my own ignorance." And it was the Apostle Paul who said, "For I am the least of the apostles" (I Corinthians 15:9). The favored people with the greatest gifts and the most usefulness do not need to brag.

As harvest time approached, a farmer and his son walked into a wheat field to inspect it. The son said, "Look here, Daddy, how straight these stalks stand, unbending, holding up their heads. Surely, they are the best ones. The others that hang their heads down must not be very good." "To the contrary," replied the father, "those that are lightheaded have no substance, no weight; that's why they are straight. The ones that are bent have heavy heads full of grain." We can learn a lesson from this. Full heads have no trouble bending low in meekness. It is the empty ones that remain with noses proudly pointed to the sky.

◆ *Understandably, the first article of peace is meekness.* It is easy for persons with a meek and quiet spirit to live in peace. Yes, they may disagree on some matters, but their meekness lets them disagree without quarreling.

> *He that is of a proud heart stirreth up strife.*
> —PROVERBS 28:25

Contrary to what the world thinks, nothing is lost by the yielding spirit of meekness. A classic example is that of Abram (who God later renamed Abraham). When his herdsmen and Lot's herdsmen quarreled because the land was overcrowded, it was the yielding spirit of Abram that caused him to propose: "Let there be no strife, I pray thee, between me and thee, and between my herdmen and thy herdmen; for we be brethren. Is not the whole land before thee? separate thyself, I pray thee, from me: if thou wilt take the left hand, then I will go to the right; or if thou depart to the right hand, then I will go to the left" (Genesis 13:8,9). You remember the rest of this oft-told story. Lot chose the well-watered plain of the Jordan and tragically landed in Sodom. However, Abram's meekness and peacefulness paid off; he never lost a thing; he never suffered the disasters of Sodom that befell poor Lot.

◆ *Furthermore, meekness will make you beautiful.* God "will beautify the meek" (Psalm 149:4). Meekness provides a calmness and peace of mind that adds to the luster of one's countenance. Inward feelings affect outward expressions. They should. And they do.

This adorable and winsome spirit is more appreciated when we consider contrasting natures. The dove is meek; the hawk is domineering; which do you like better? The house cat is meek; the tiger is overbearing; which do you prefer? One person is meek; another is lordly; which one do you favor? We are all agreed on meekness. Isn't it marvelous and encouraging that meek people without trying receive more appreciation and acclaim than the swaggering swell heads who try so hard for a place in the world? So if you want esteem and goodwill, be mild rather than proud, and be mild rather than brutish.

◆ *Now, it is easy to see* why "the meek...shall inherit the earth" (Matthew 5:5). It was John Woolman who said, "Selfish men may possess the earth; it is the meek only who inherit it from the Heavenly Father, free from all the defilements and perplexities of unrighteousness." How wonderful!

GARDENS OF THE HEART

SELF-CONTROL

SELF-CONTROL

GARDENS OF THE HEART

What is self-control?

What does it mean?

What is its real and full significance?

# 9  SELF-CONTROL

In a wide sense it means the mastery over all evil tendencies and denotes moderation in one's whole manner of living. There is no higher adventure than the control of self. And no greater success.

◆ *Self-control is opposed* to debauchery, gluttony, lust, drunkenness, gossip, outbursts of temper, spite, and additionally: even good things when pursued to excess, for instance work, play and thrift.

1) We are commanded:

*Wherefore, my beloved brethren,*
*let every man be swift to hear, slow to speak,*
*slow to wrath.*
—JAMES 1:19

And that is self-control.

2) Jesus laid down this rule of behavior:

*But whosoever shall smite thee on thy right cheek,
turn to him the other also.*
—MATTHEW 5:39

And that is self-control.

3) Solomon stated:

*When thou sittest to eat with a ruler, consider
diligently what is before thee: And put a knife
to thy throat, if thou be a man given to appetite.*
—PROVERBS 23:1,2

And that is self-control.

4) The Apostle Paul said:

*And be not drunk with wine, wherein is excess; but
be filled with the Spirit.*
—EPHESIANS 4:18

And that is self-control.

5) Paul has further spoken:

*This I say then, Walk in the Spirit, and ye shall not
fulfil the lust of the flesh.*
—GALATIANS 5:16

And that is self-control.

◆ *Furthermore, the last two passages tell us how*

*self-control is accomplished.* They inform us that it is a Spirit-related matter. "Be filled with the Spirit." "Walk in the Spirit." Inasmuch as self-control is a fruit of the Spirit, we would expect this. For when the Spirit's teachings imbibe our inner being, self-control is a natural fruit.

And if the fruit of one's religion is not self-mastery, then there must be something wrong with that person's religion. For self-control is one of the basics of life. Indeed, unless you rule yourself, you will be ruled by others and circumstances. There can be no sovereign power apart from self-control.

> *Self-reverence, self-knowledge, self-control,*
> *These three alone lead life to sovereign power.*
> —ALFRED TENNYSON

◆ *This being true, then the person who controls himself attains the highest accomplishment* and thus is the mightiest hero. This is the point Solomon made:

> *He that ruleth his spirit [is greater] than he that taketh a city.*
> —PROVERBS 16:32

This proverb was written at a time when it was considered to be a maximum achievement to conquer and sack a city. After a city had been stormed by an invading army, leaving blood, smoke, death, and devastation in its wake, then the conqueror made his triumphal parade, mounted on a prancing, colorfully adorned steed, or in a dazzling, gilded chariot. There were the hurrahs of the victors and the hushes of the vanquished. Quite a paradox. Yet it was looked upon as the most notable and momentous exploit of man. But there is a feat that is greater. Self-control. He that rules himself is greater than he that takes a city.

> *He who reigns within himself and rules his passions,*
> *desires and fears, is more than a king.*
> —JOHN MILTON

◆ *Every person needs to be in complete control of himself,* not a puppet on a string manipulated by another person, or by drink, or by appetite, or by an uncontrollable temper.

> *For a man to conquer himself*
> *is the first and noblest of all virtues.*
> —PLATO

By being the master of yourself you are the master of your fate.

The man taken to the little town clinic was battered, bruised and suffering from a broken leg. What happened? He lost control of a team of horses, they ran away, and he was thrown from the wagon. Horses out of control are dangerous; so is a fire, so is a locomotive; but, the greatest menace of all is a person out of control. He is his worst enemy.

◆ *The intemperate are not free.* Their own intemperance has enslaved them in the cruelest kind of bondage. It happened because they thought they were having a good time. But they were deceived. For there is much more joy in being the master than in being the servant.

While I recognize the greed and graspingness behind the liquor traffic, I have no ill will—none whatsoever—toward those engaged in it, though I do dislike what they are doing. For I hate intemperate alcohol, and because I believe I have good reasons:

> —*I detest it for the human suffering it has caused.*
> —*I abhor it for the human wrecks it has produced.*
> —*I loathe it for the poverty it has heaped on millions.*
> —*I resent it for the mental institutions it has peopled.*
> —*I dislike it for the homes it has destroyed.*
> —*I detest it for the moral decay it has fostered.*
> —*I despise it for the countless graves it has filled in potter's fields and on boothills.*

Truly "wine is a mocker, strong drink is raging" (Proverbs 20:1). How can anyone love that which is so fraught with misery? No one, except the person who has lost control of himself.

◆ *While a superb reason for self-control* is the blessings it brings now, the most impelling and rewarding motive for it is the incorruptible crown.

Centuries ago along a beautiful avenue in Corinth were marble tablets of the athletic contests. For one to have his name there was an outstanding distinction. So it was the fervent ambition of every athlete in Greece to have his name inscribed on one of those tablets. Athletes did not receive the financial rewards then as today, but the glory was just as great then as now. Maybe more, for the honor was his only pay. To obtain that fame, the athlete subjected himself for several months to the most strenuous discipline, training and self-control. At the climax of his training and preparation, he entered the contest and strove for mastery. It was that temperance and training that Paul used as an example to teach a spiritual lesson, as follows:

> *And every man that striveth for the mastery is temperate in all things. Now they do it to obtain a corruptible crown; but we an incorruptible.*
> —I CORINTHIANS 9:25